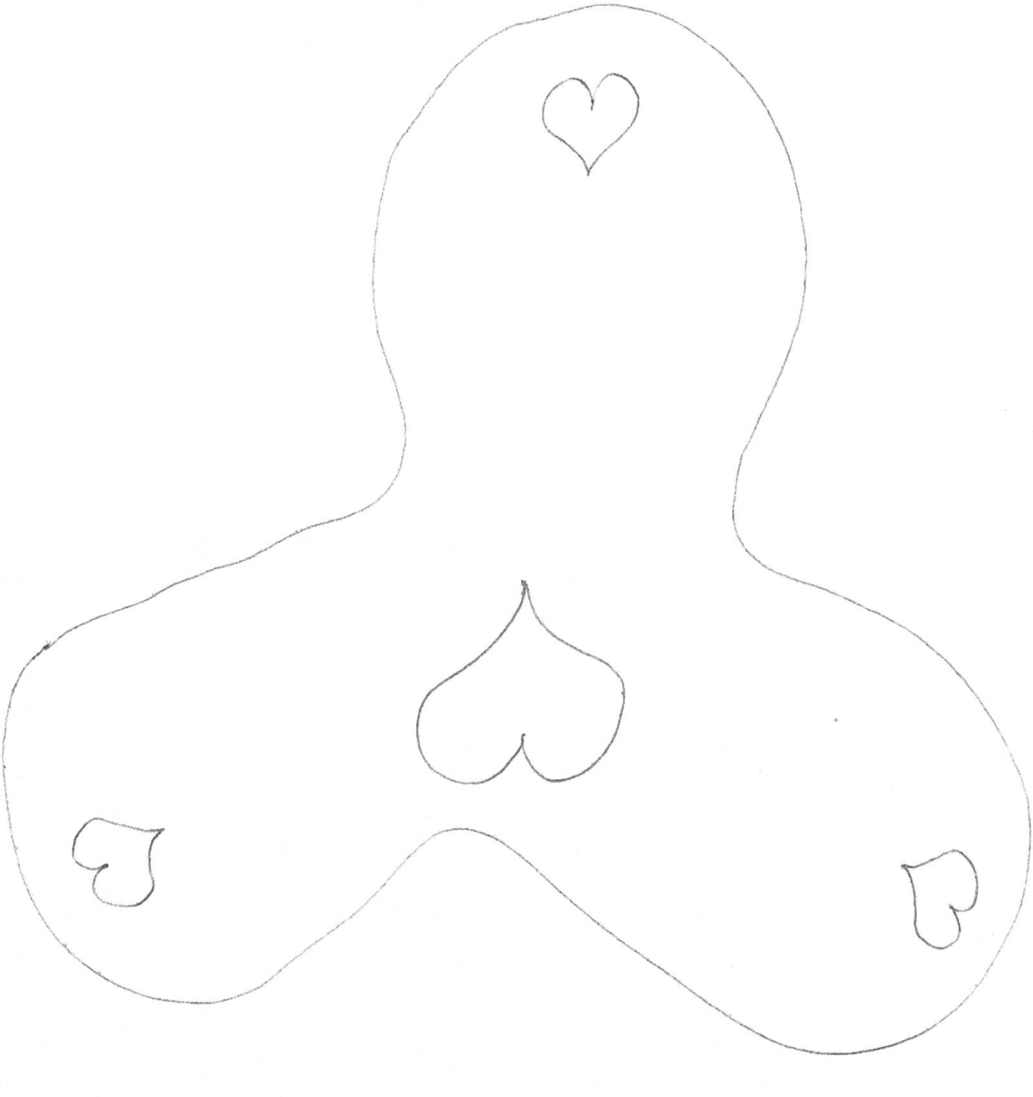

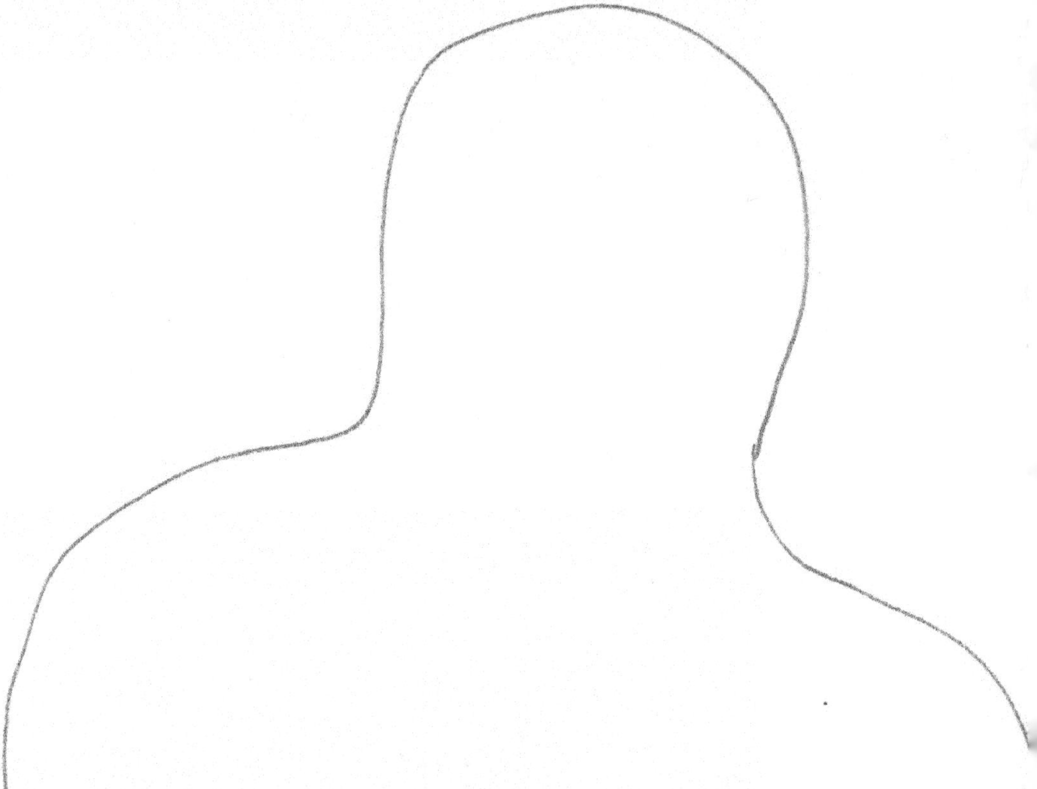

Thank you

for your

Support in our

futures.

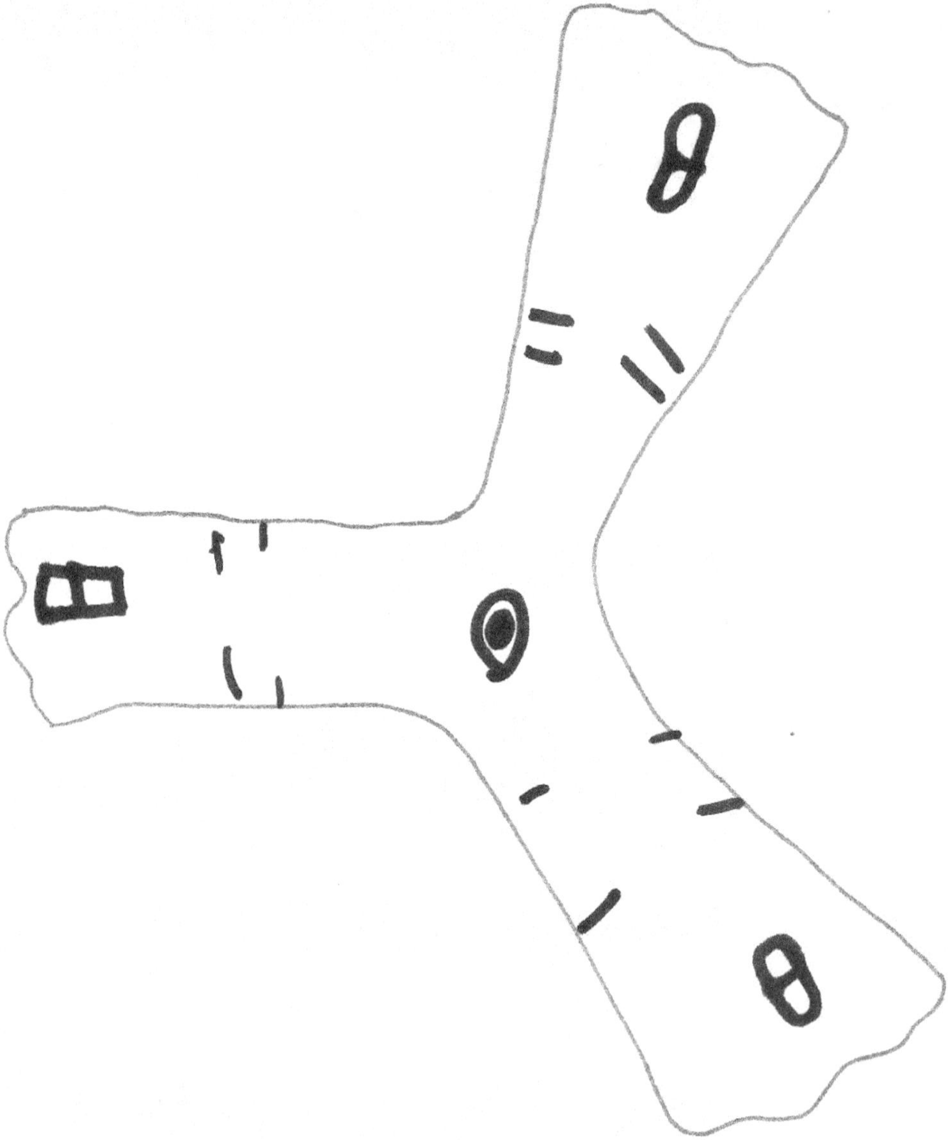

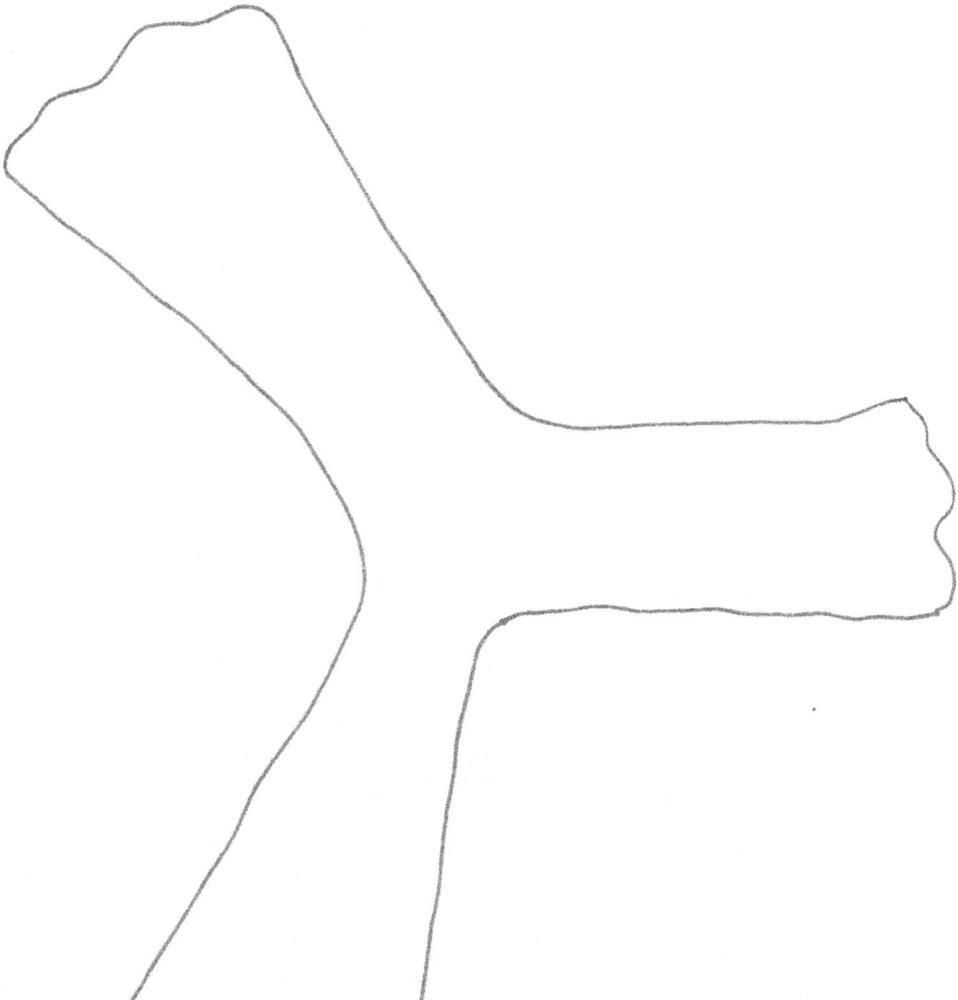

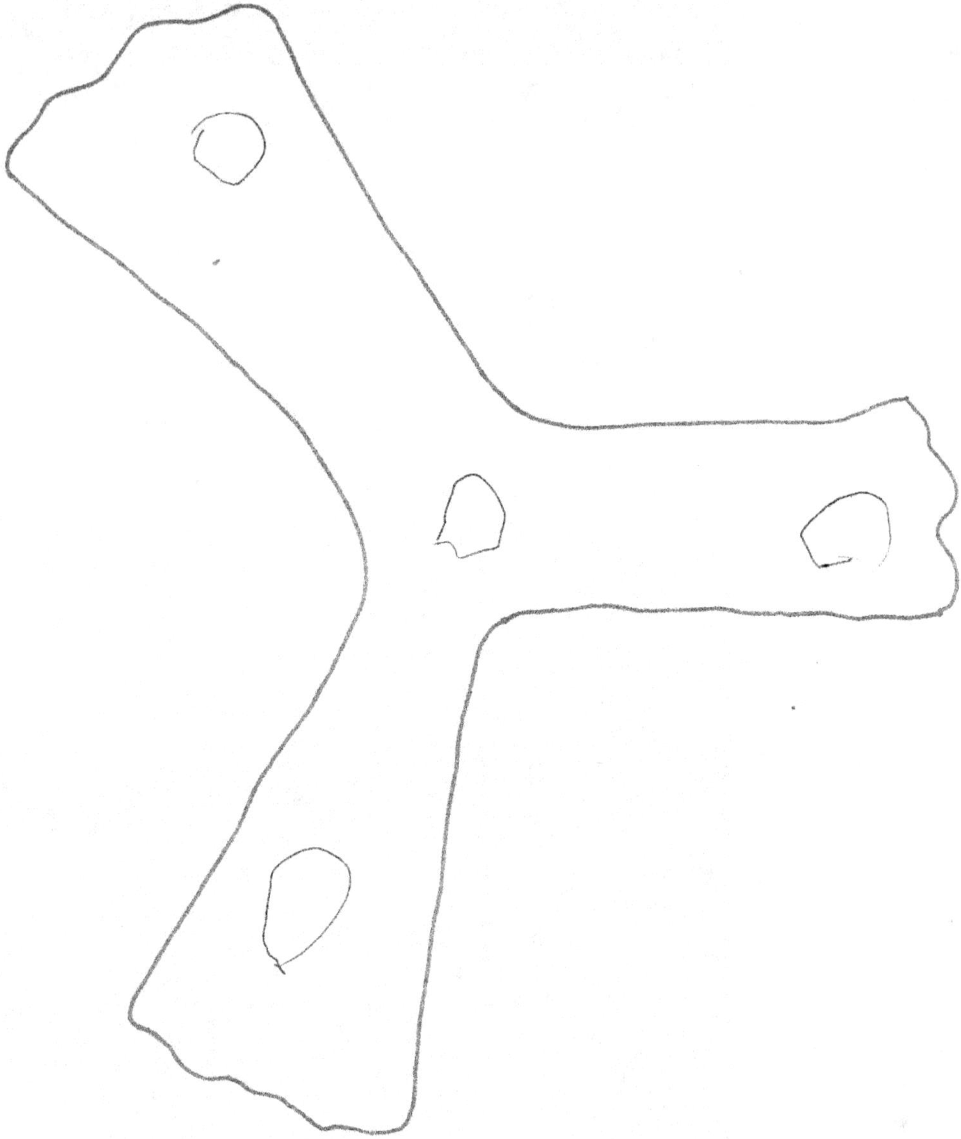

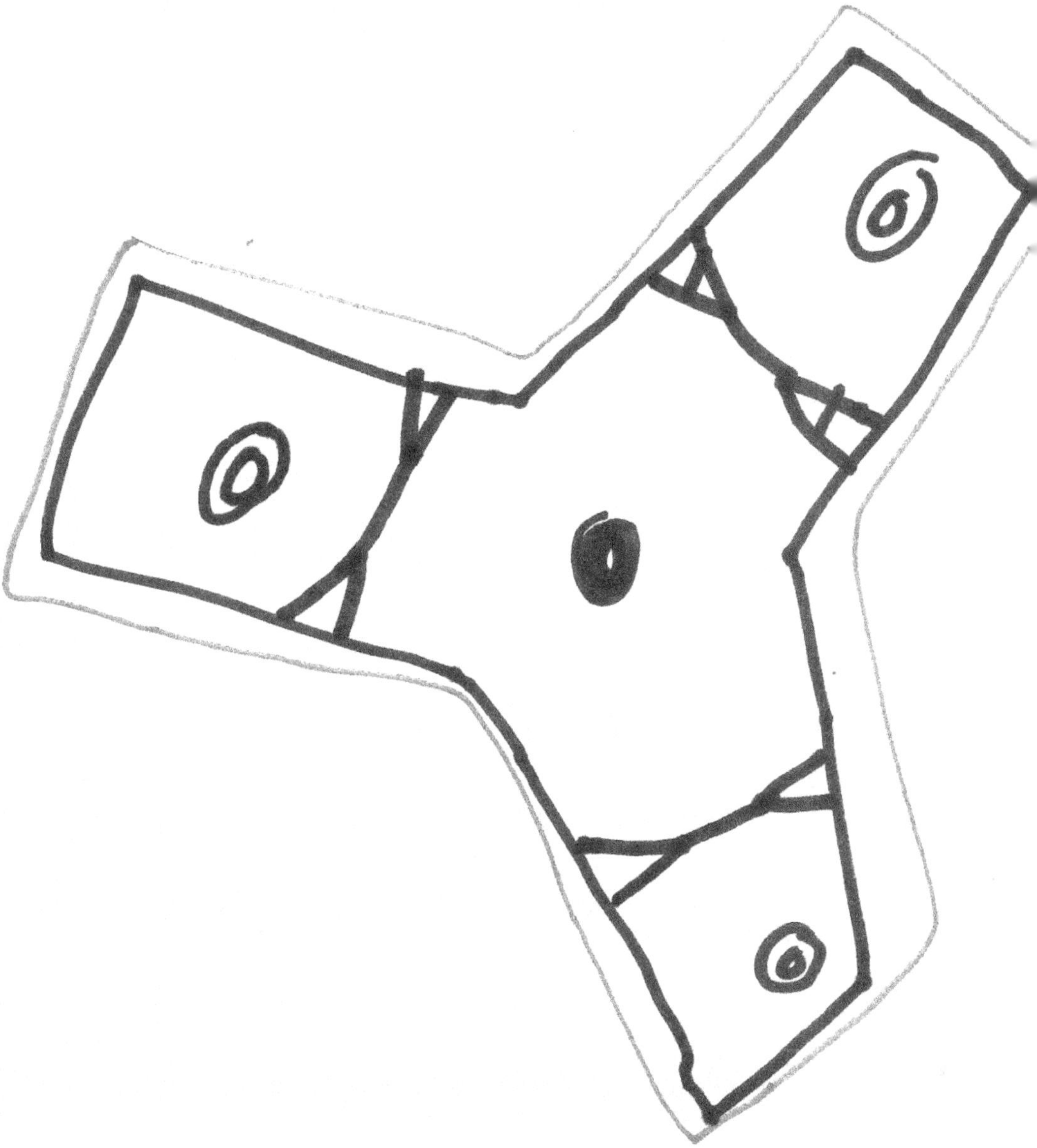

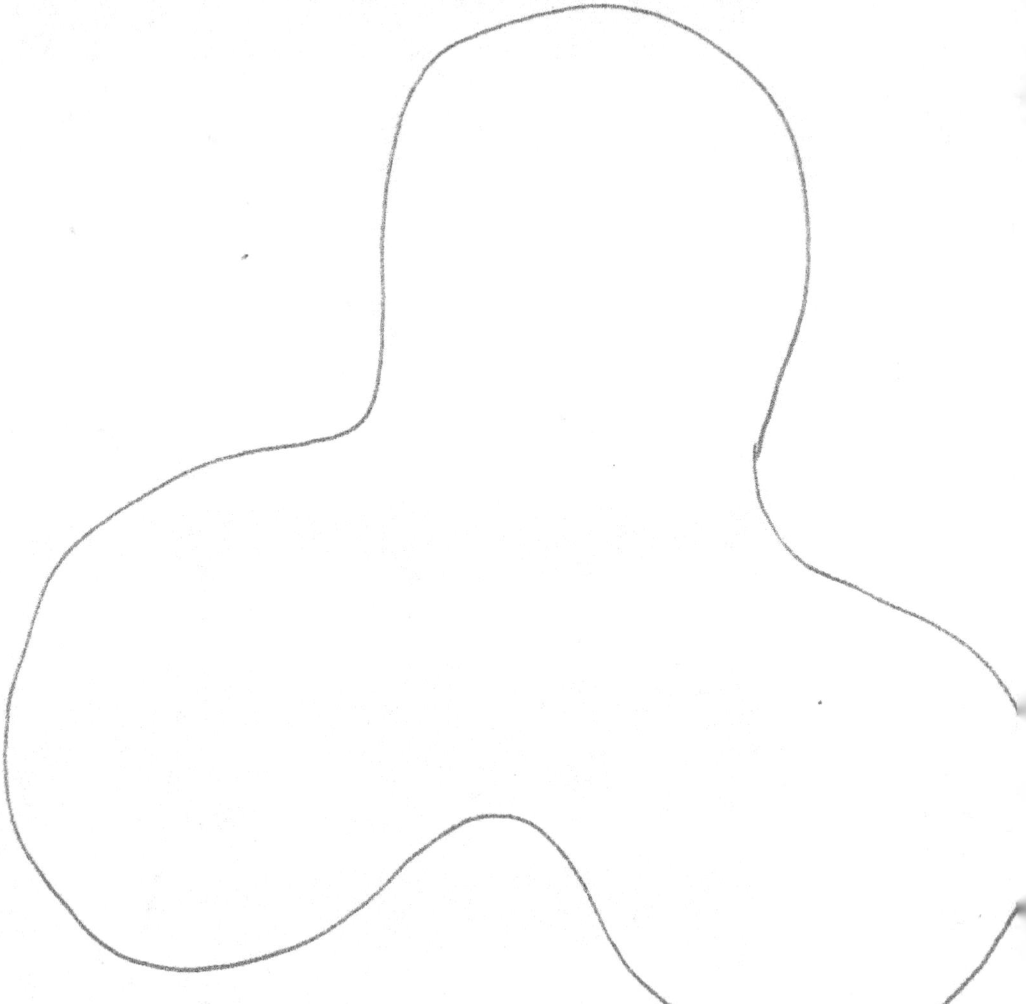

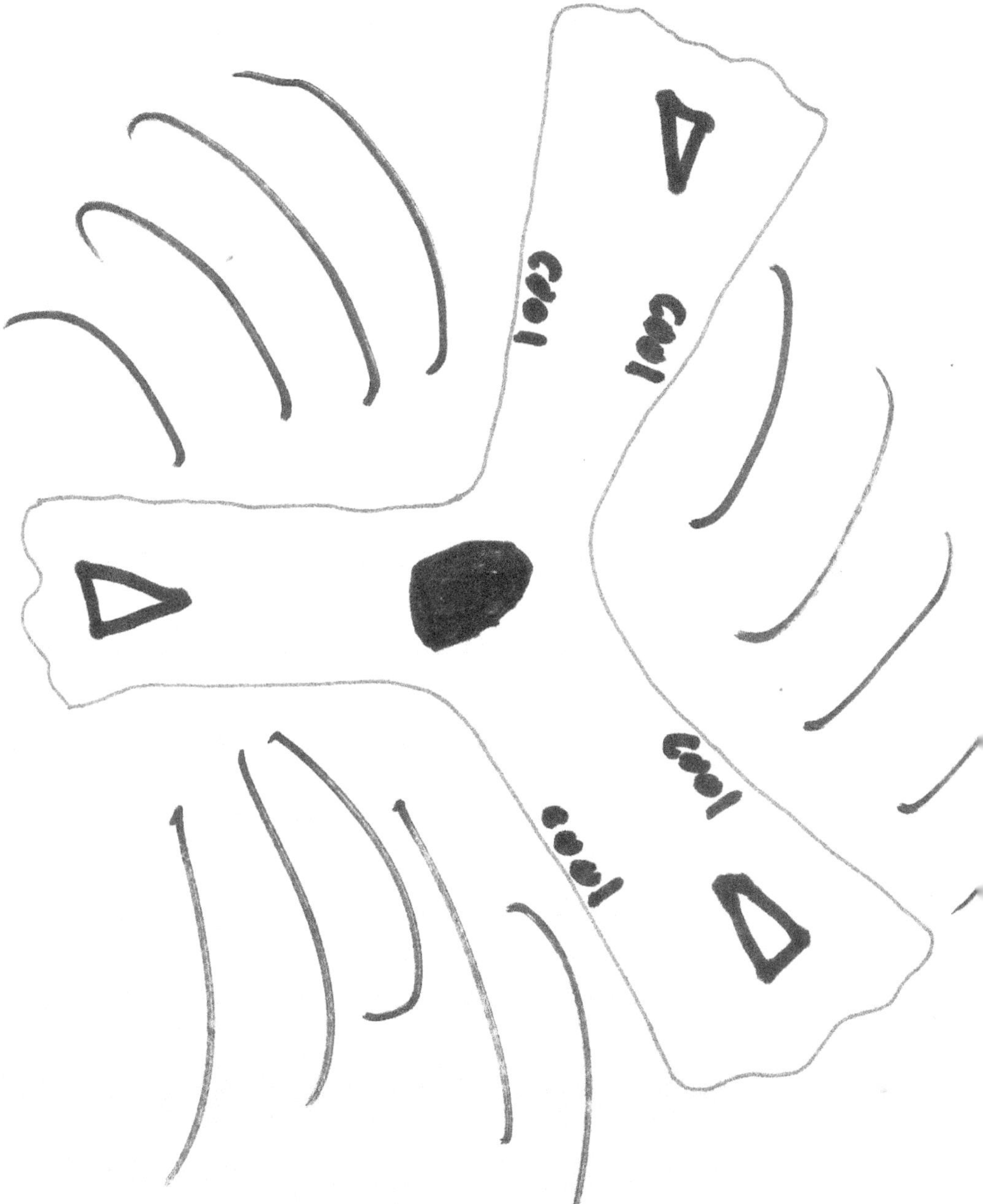
Cool
Cool
Cool
cool

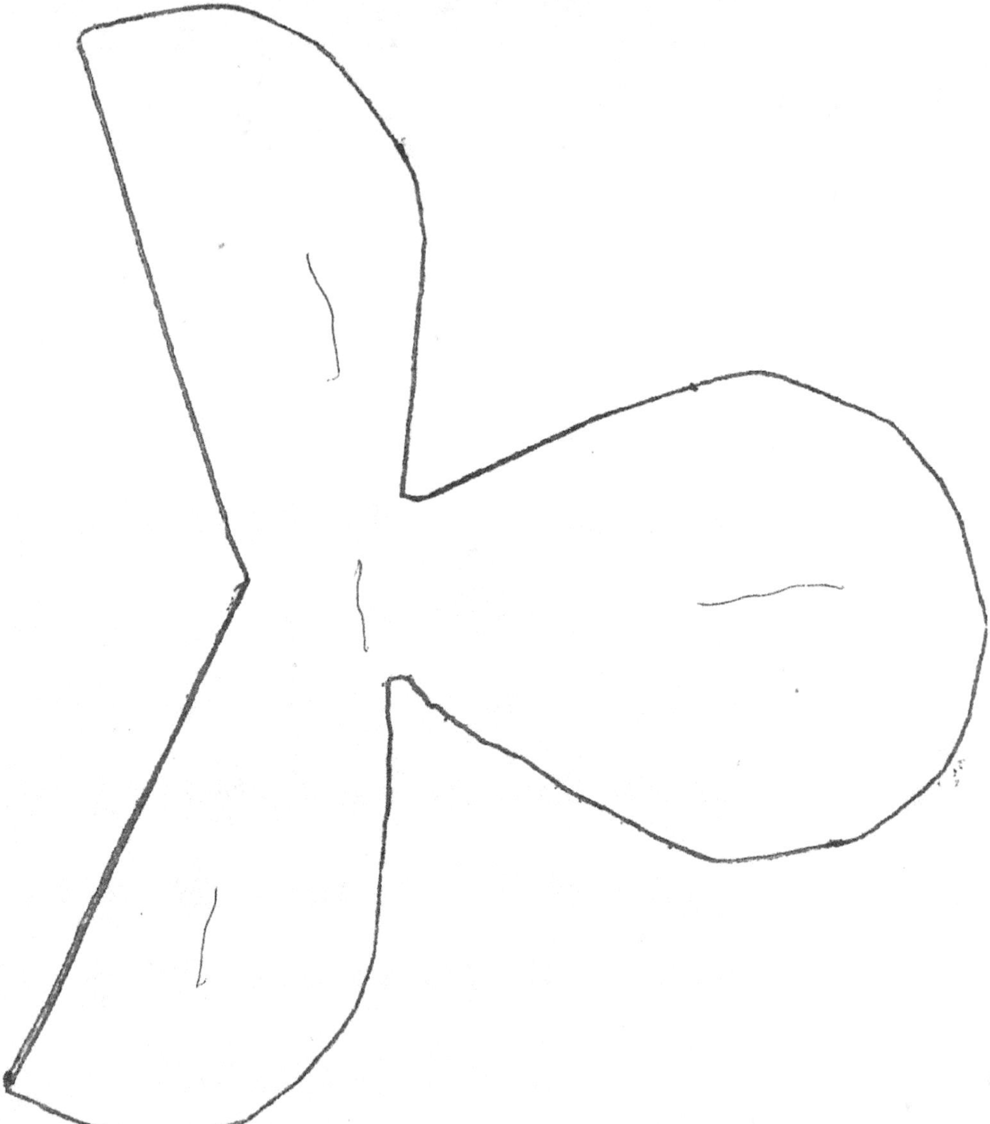

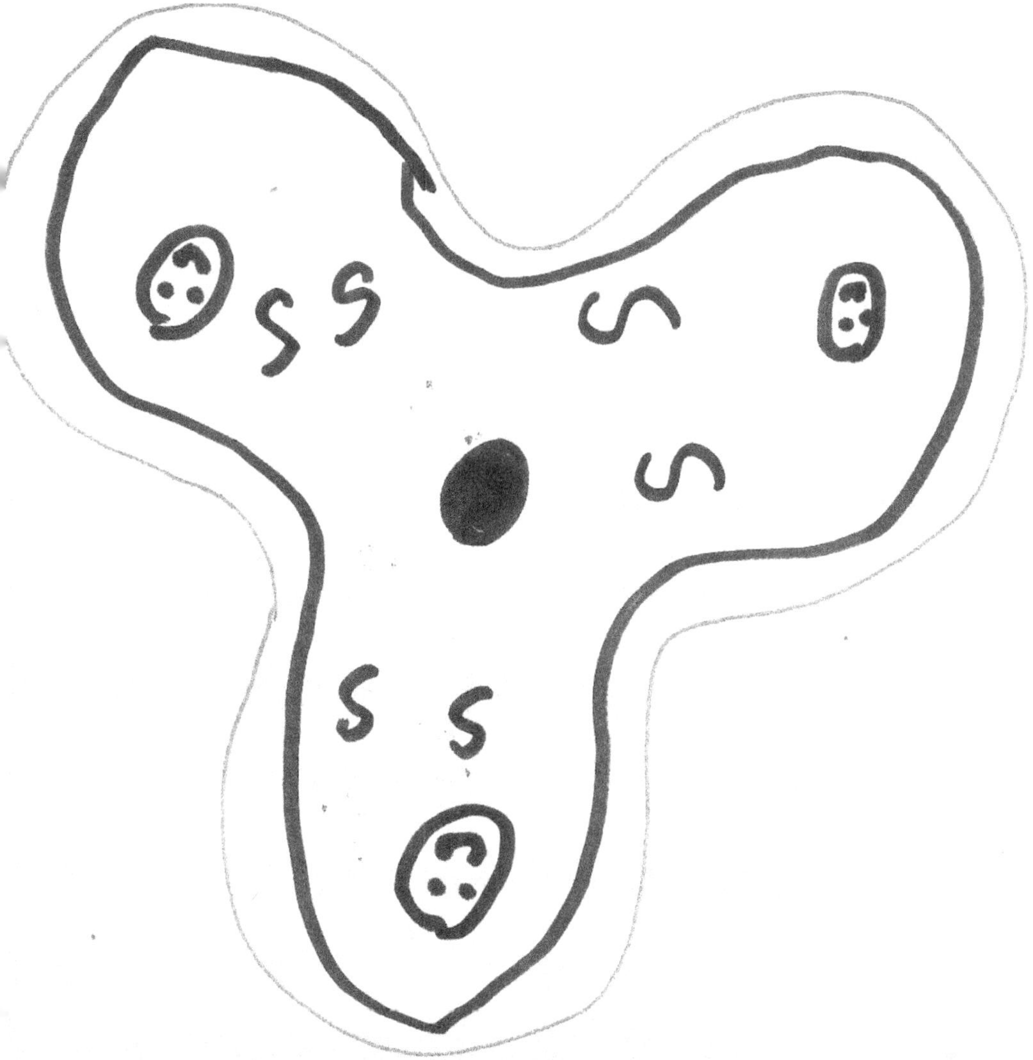

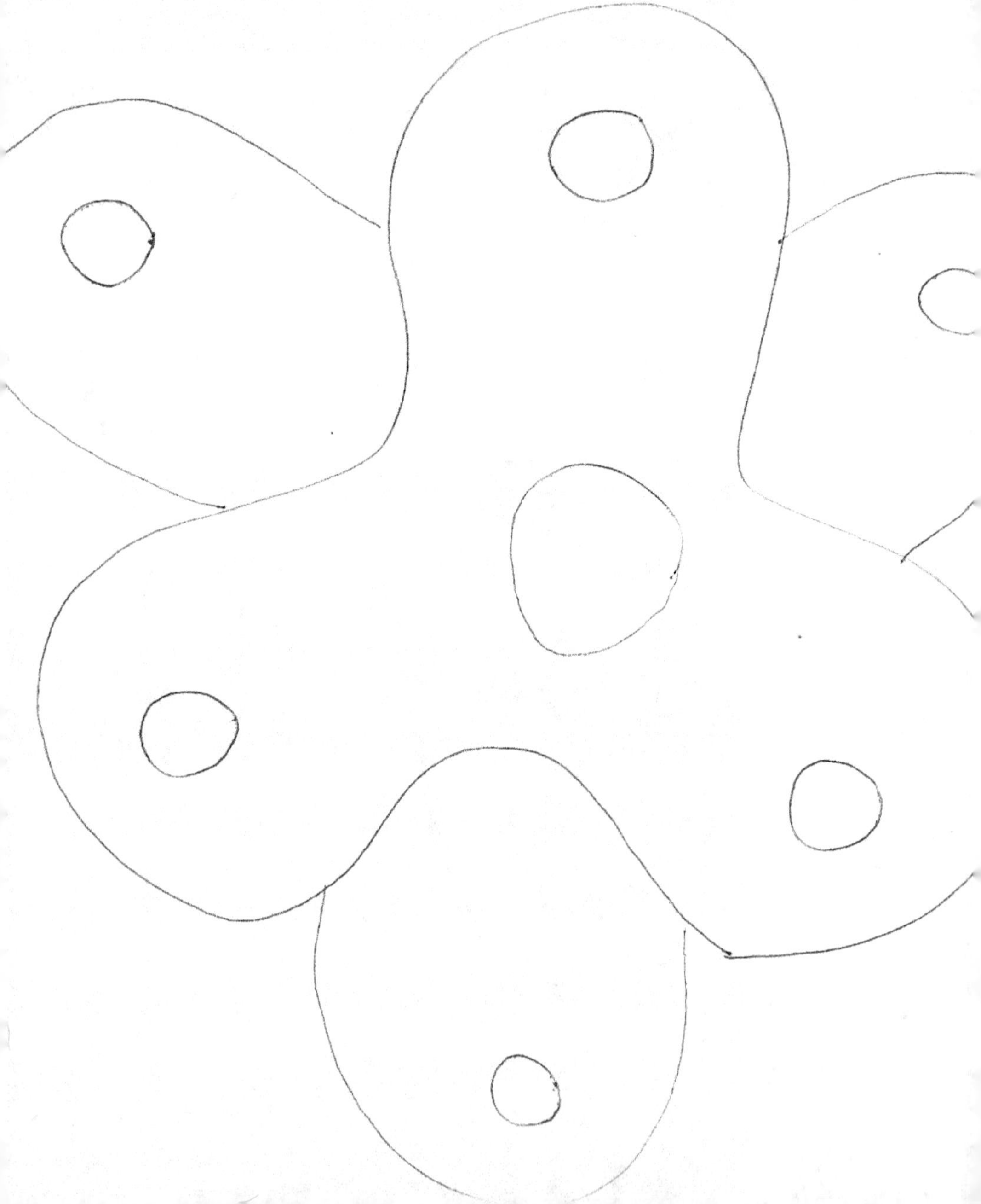

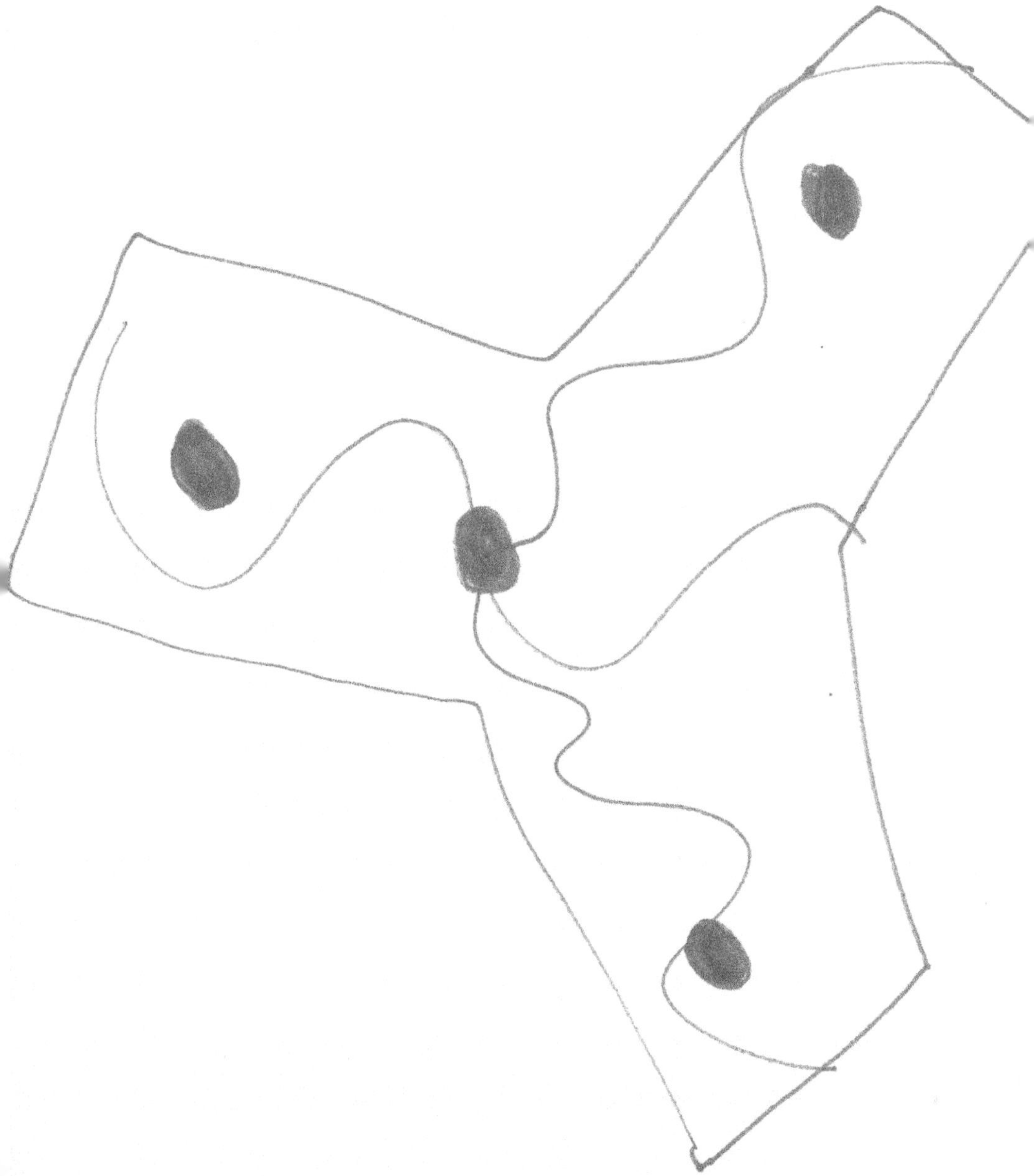

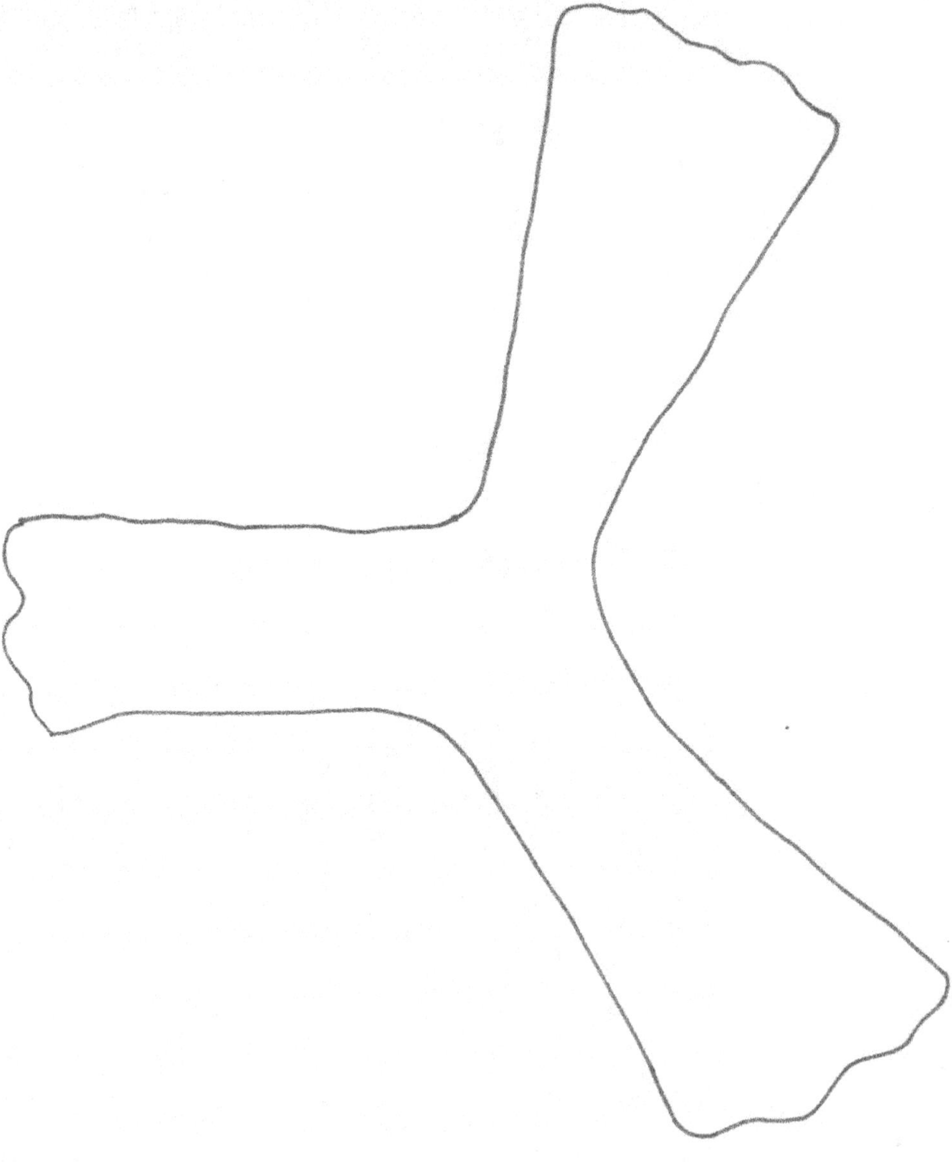

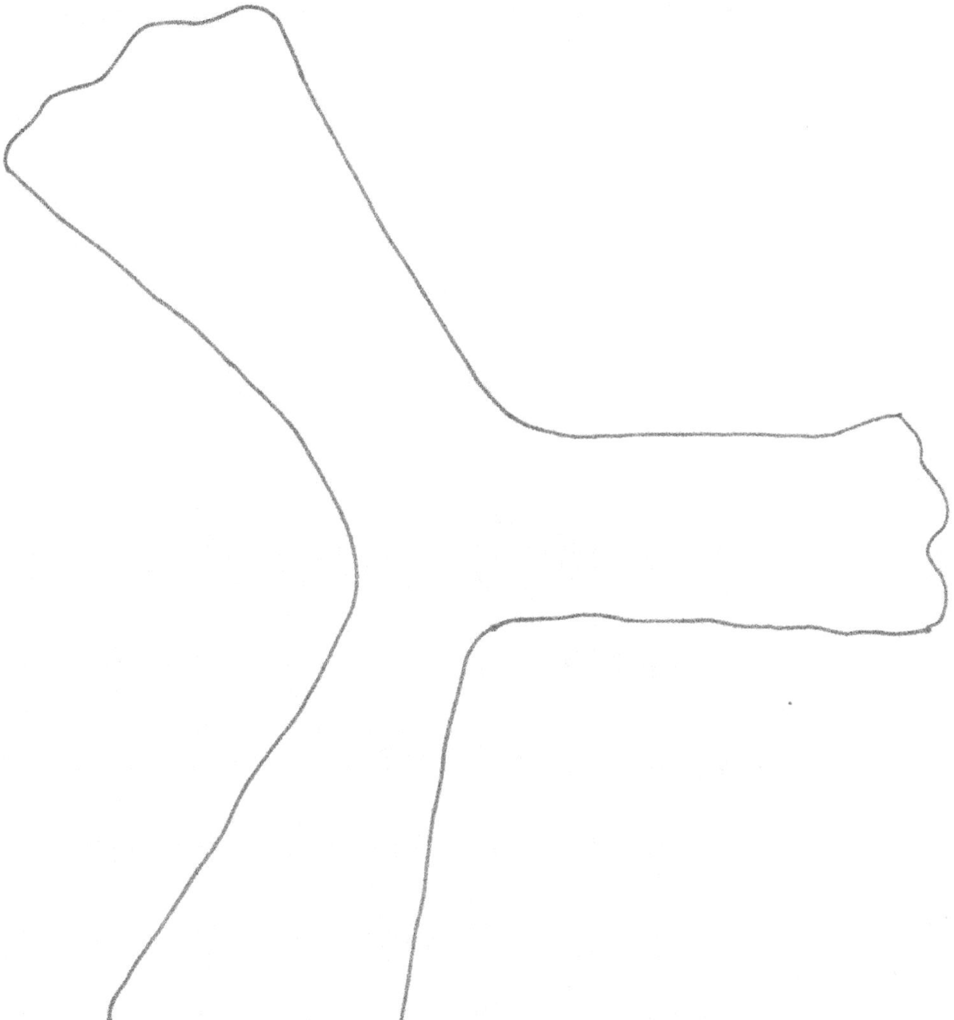

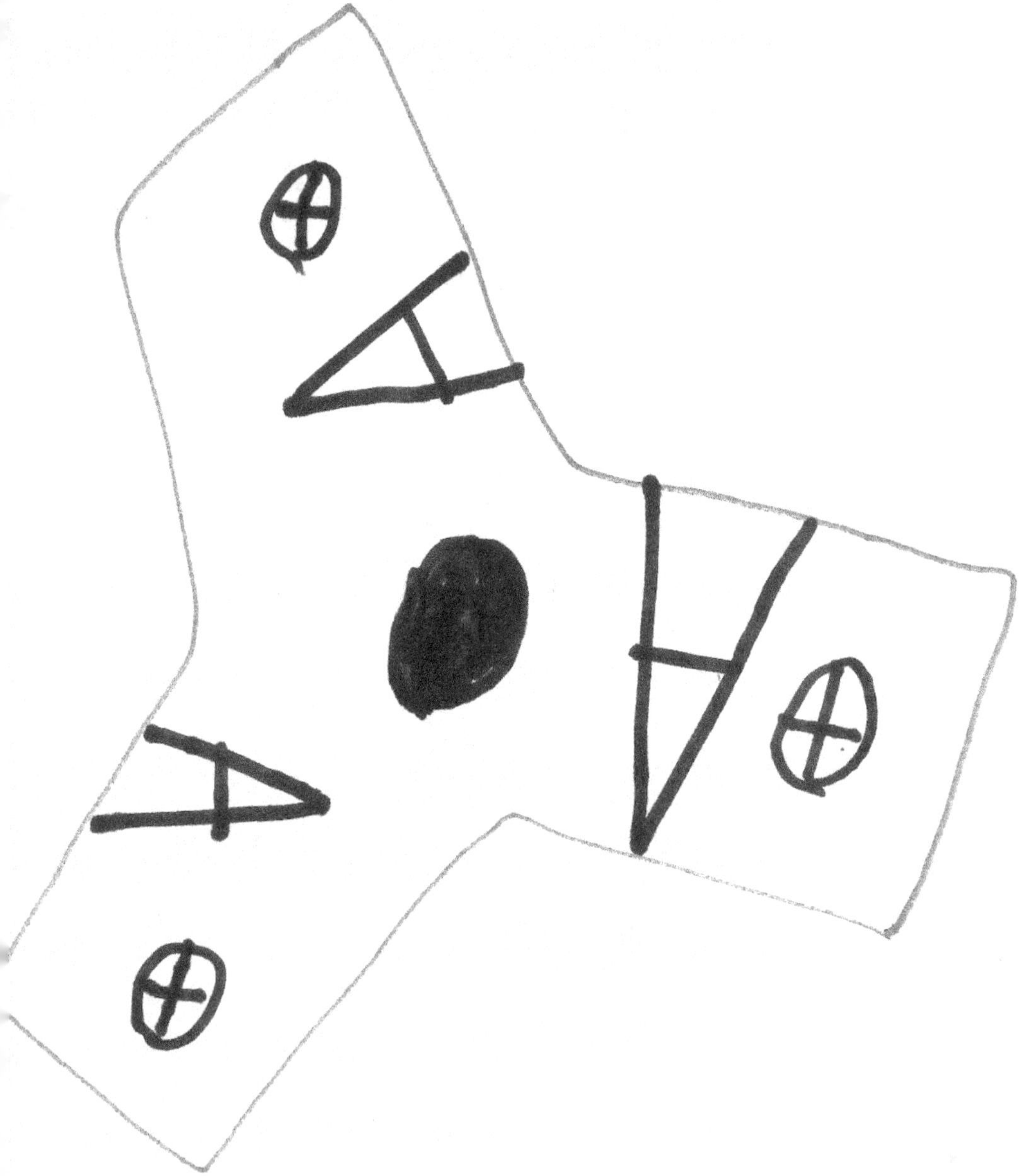

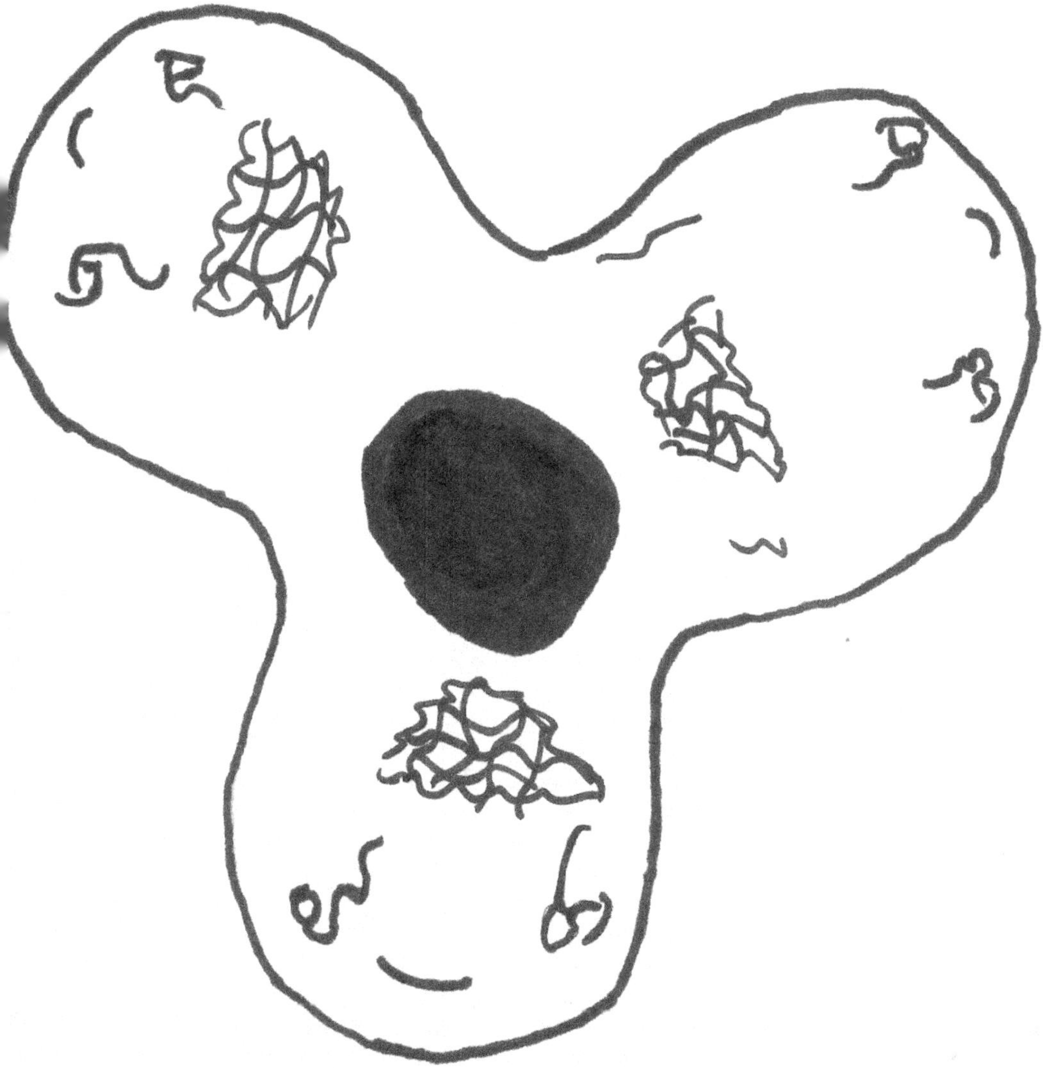

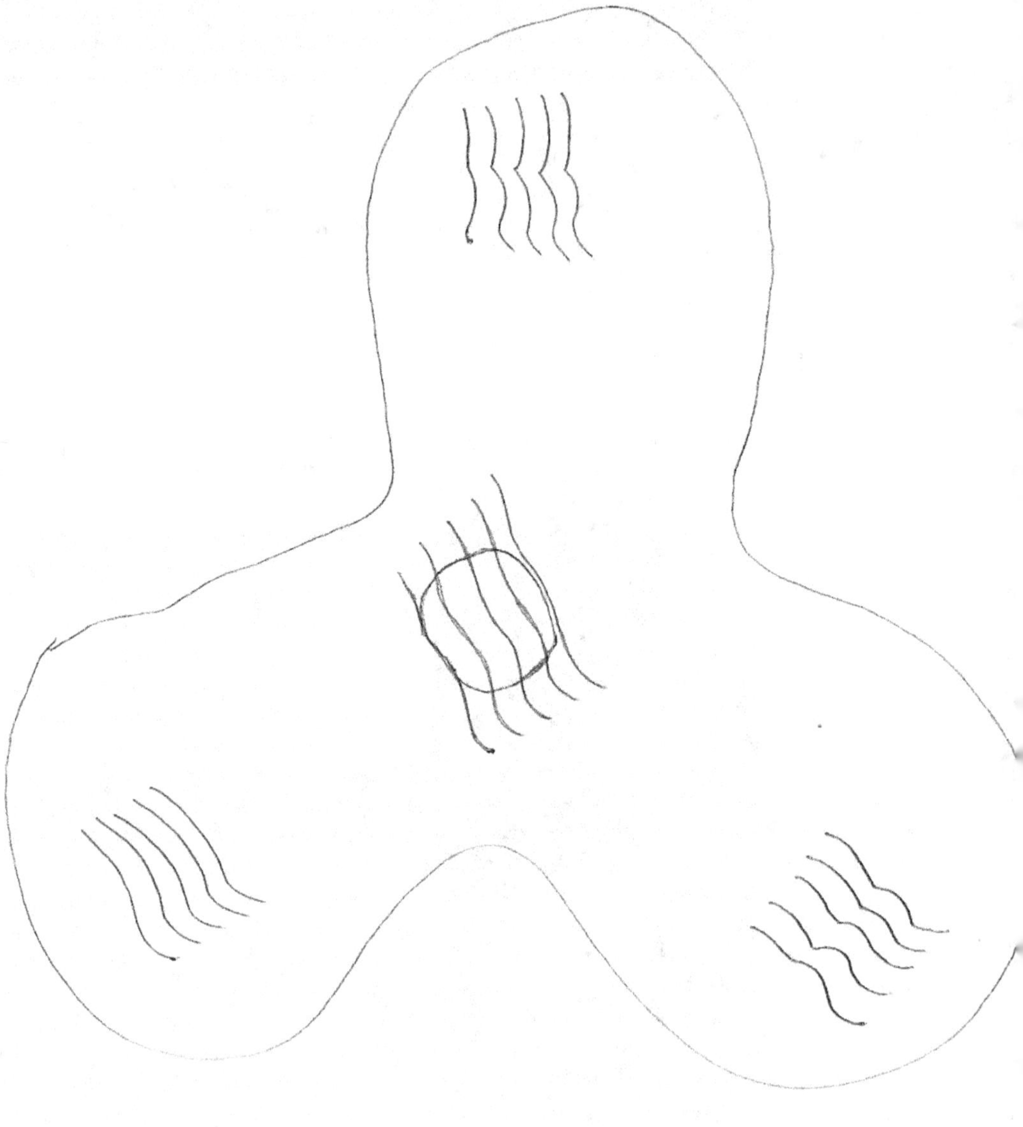

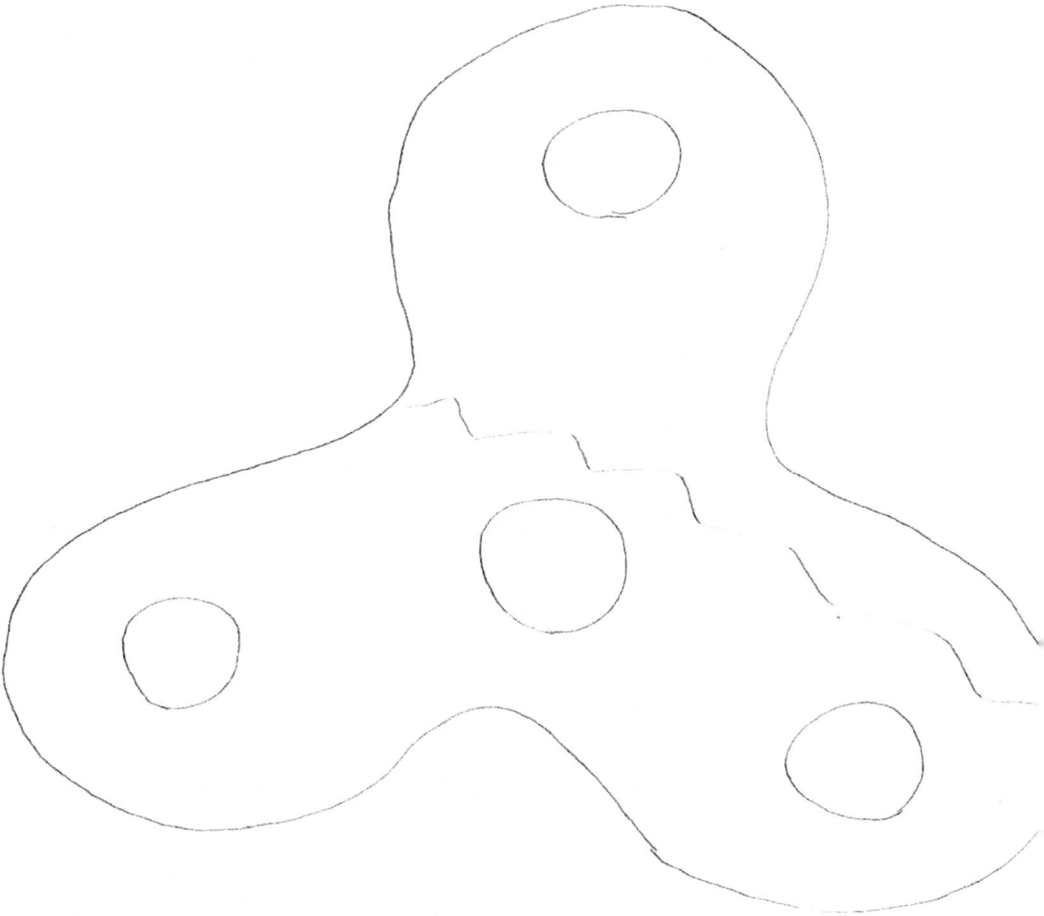

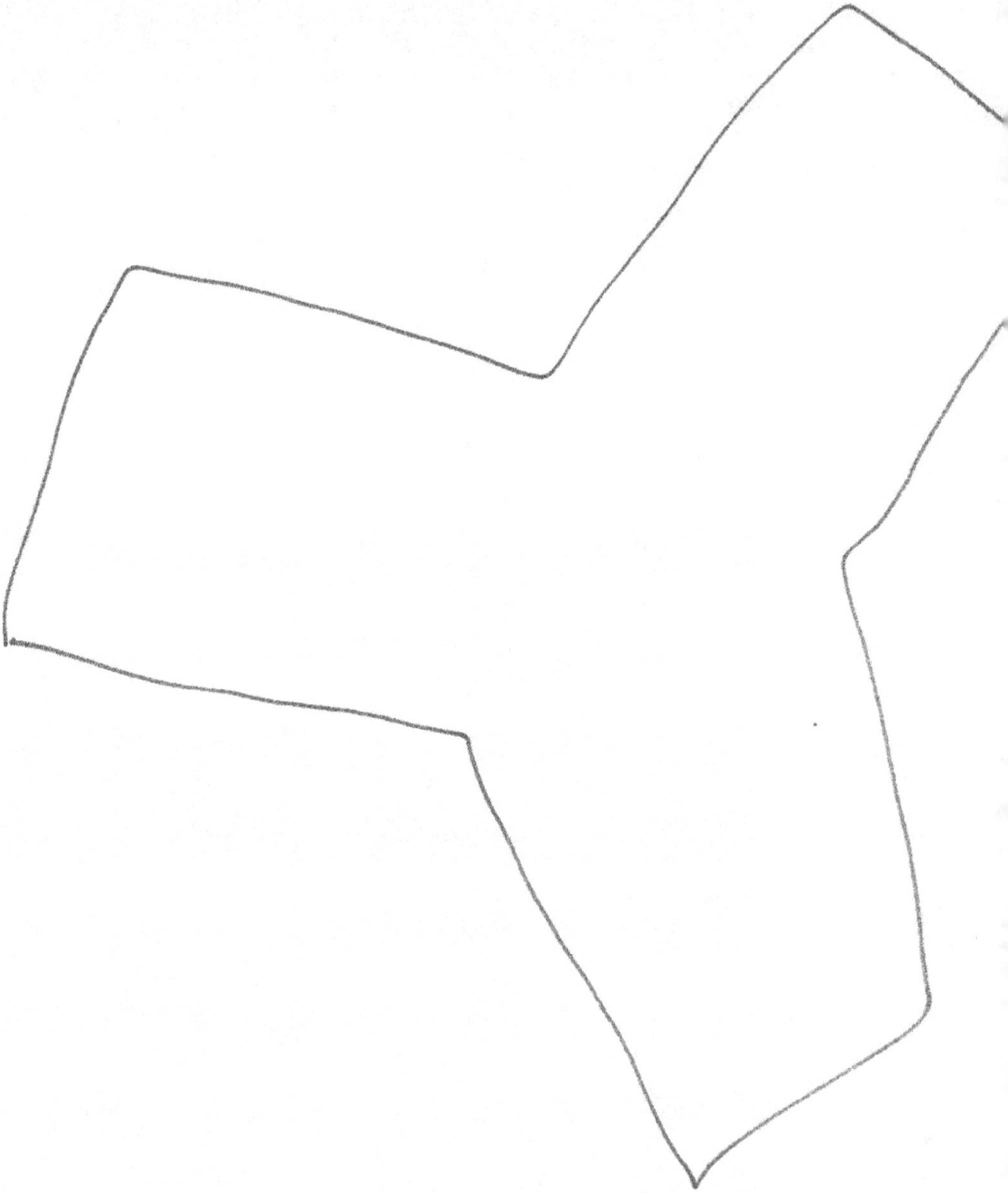

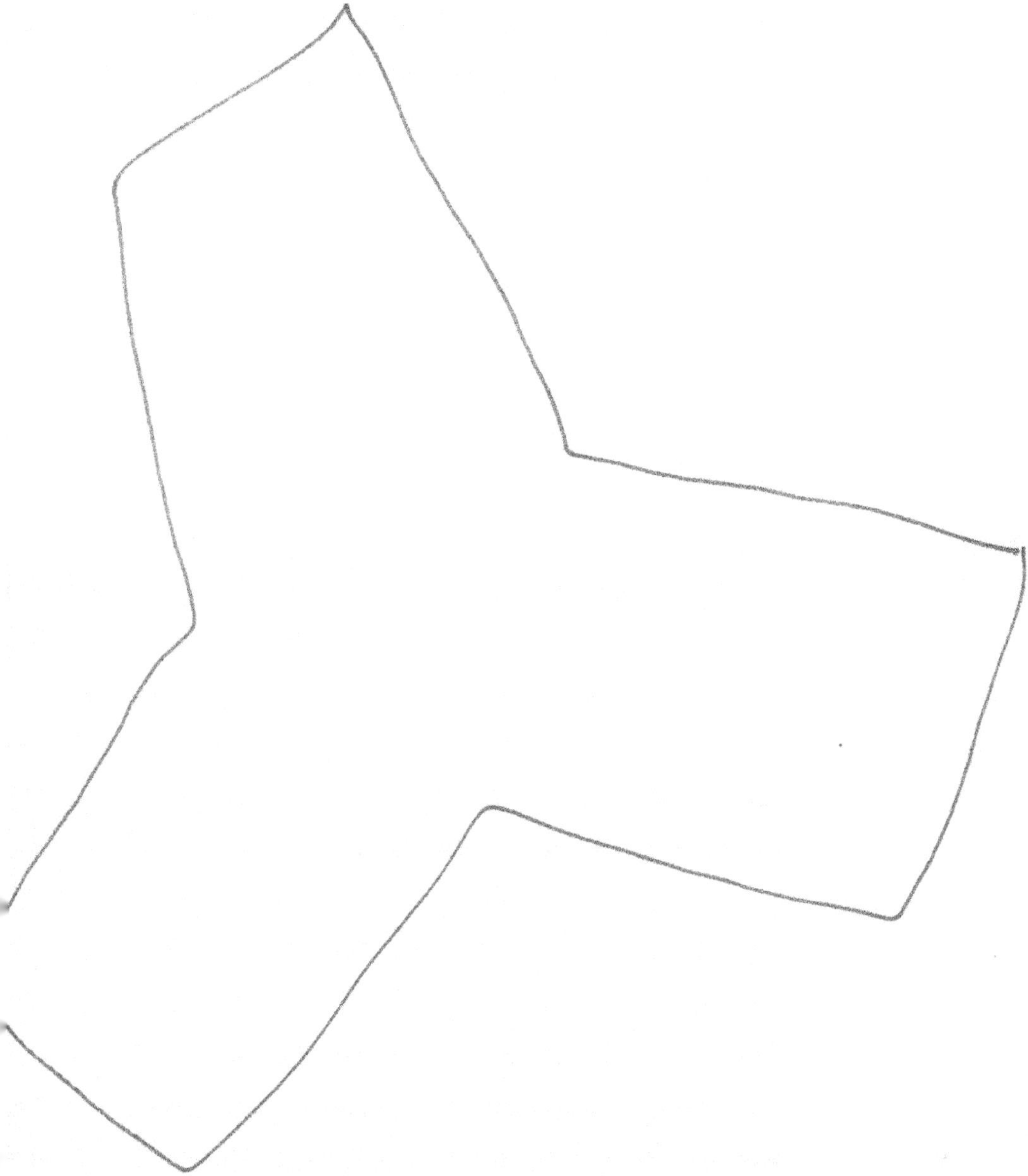

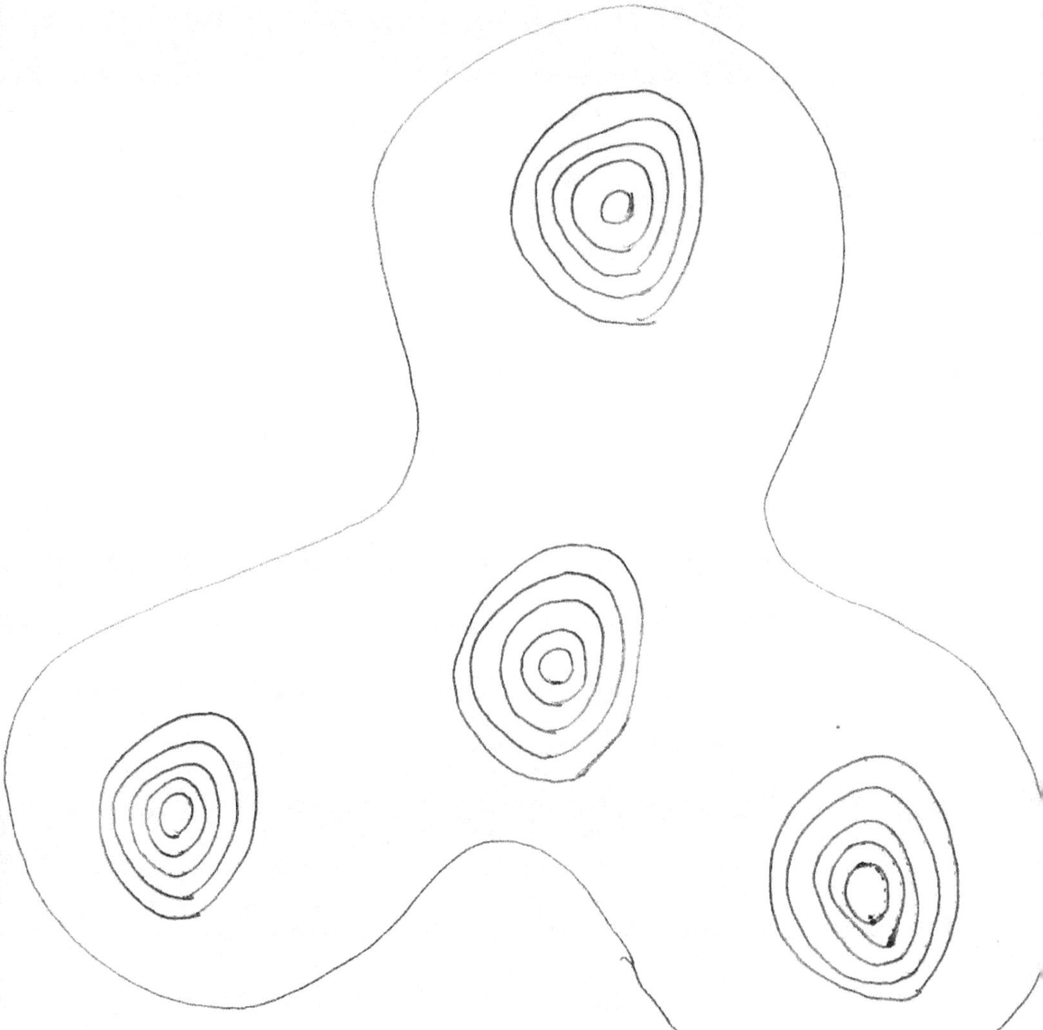

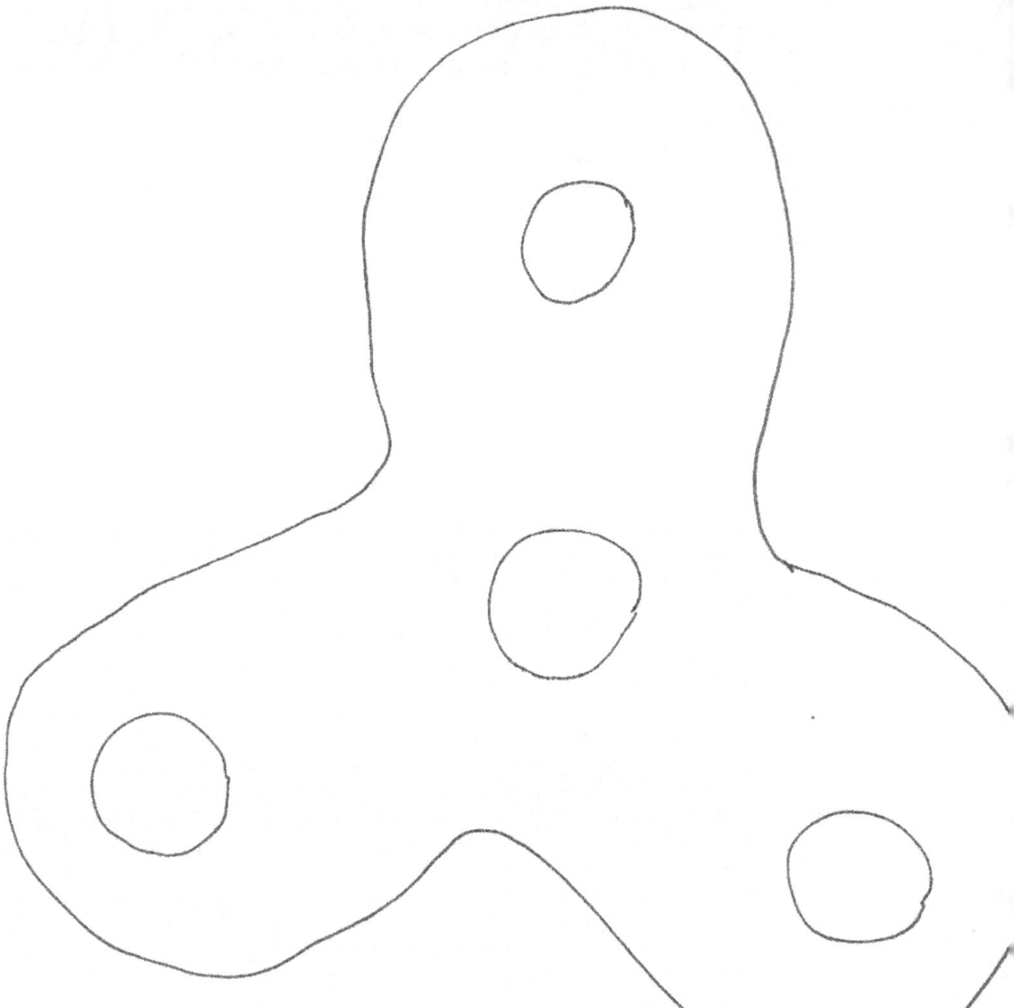

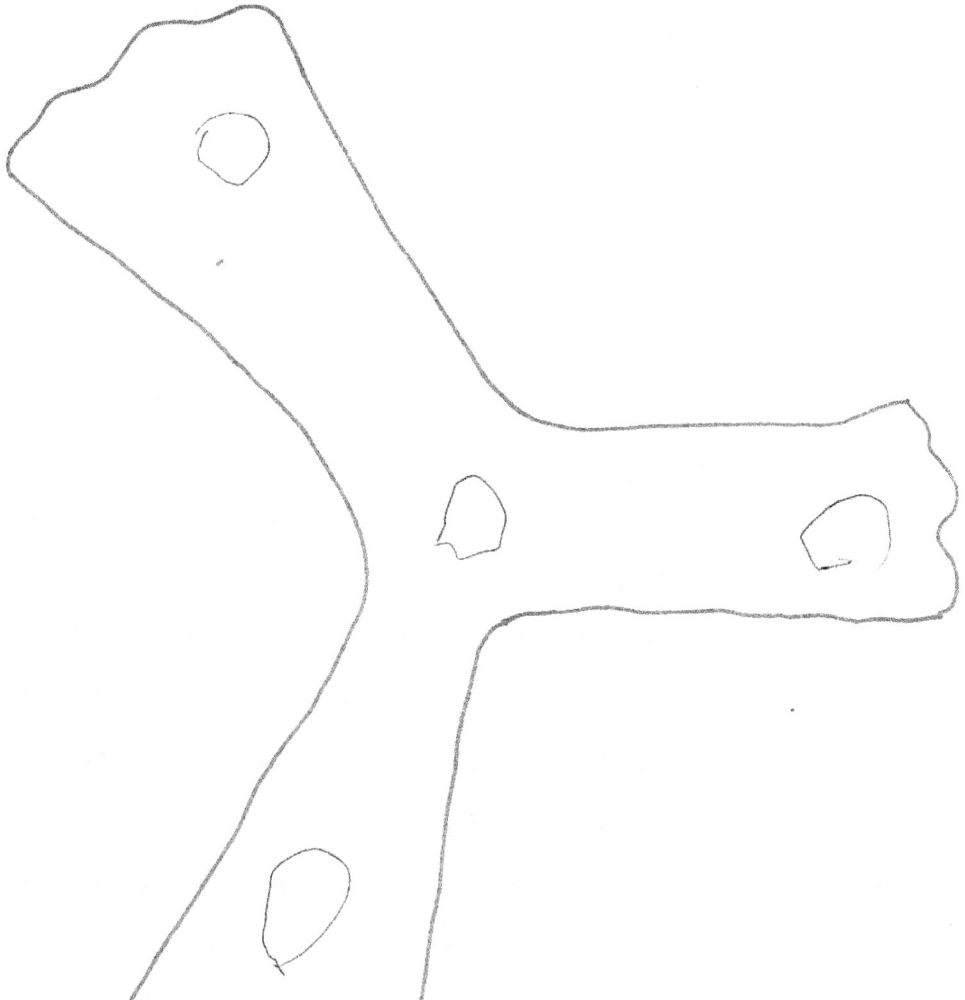

www.ingramcontent.com/pod-product-compliance
Lightning Source LLC
Chambersburg PA
CBHW050039230526
45470CB00003B/1354